CW00400208

BELIEVE

Confess

FOR TEENS

BY VICTORIA COOPER

Copyright © Victoria Cooper 2021
First edition printed 2021.
All rights reserved. No part of this publication may be reproduced, stored in a retrieval system, or transmitted in any form or by means, electronic, mechanical, photocopying or otherwise, without the prior written consent of the publisher. Short extracts may be used for review purposes.

Unless indicated, Scripture quotations are taken from The Holy Bible, New International Version®, NIV®, Copyright © 1973, 1978, 1984, 2011 by Biblica, Inc. ®
Used by permission. All rights reserved worldwide.

Graphic Design by Victoria Cooper
Images from Pixabay

ISBN: 9798716718586

OTHER BOOKS BY VICTORIA COOPER
A Fusion of Humanity & Divinity
Believe & Confess For Kids
STRONGER: 40 Day Devotional
Believe & Confess

DEDICATION

I want to dedicate this book to every Sunday School teacher, youth leader
& pastor who taught me the Bible, introduced me to the Holy Spirit,
showed me how to pray and encouraged me in my walk with Jesus.
This book would not exist if it wasn't for you. Thank you!

CONTENTS

INTRODUCTION

In 2019, in a vision I saw an army rising up out of the Church, but it wasn't an army of adults, it was an army of youth, 18 years and younger. They looked strong and fearless, ready for battle and eager to win. My heart skipped a beat with fear. Why are they fighting? They are innocent. Everything in me wanted to protect them.

But I felt the Spirit of God stop me in my tracks and say, *'NO! You can't protect them by cocooning them. You protect them by teaching them to fight. To fight fear! To fight anxiety! To fight worry. To fight with faith. To fight with truth in this darkening age.'*

And this is what this book is about...teaching you to fight with the Word of God.

Today, I see the progressive, constant overload from the media bombarding young people on a daily basis, putting pressure on you to accept and embrace current trends in relationships and sex, image and identity, language and attitudes.

I believe we are living in the "last days" as the Bible puts it, and it's interesting to read the apostle Paul's advice to his young spiritual son, in 2 Timothy 3.

"...evil men and (deceivers) will progress from bad to worse, deceived and deceiving, as they lead people further from the truth. Yet you must continue to advance in strength with the truth wrapped around your heart, being assured by God that he's the One who has truly taught you all these things." 2 Tim 3:13-14 (TPT)

He then goes on to say,

"Remember what you were taught from your childhood from the Holy Scriptures which can impart to you wisdom to experience everlasting life through the faith of Jesus, the Anointed One! Every Scripture has been written by the Holy Spirit, the breath of God. It will empower you by its instruction and correction, giving you the strength to take the right direction and lead you deeper into the path of godliness. Then you will be God's servant, fully mature and perfectly prepared to fulfill any assignment God gives you." 2 Tim 3:15-17

I want this book to empower you and help you to delve deeper into the scriptures. To know what God's Word says about you so when you are faced with issues of identity, you look at what God's Word says about you and not your Instagram feed.

Deuteronomy 6:7 talks about not just reading God's Word but the importance of getting it inside of you.

"Write these commandments that I've given you today on your hearts. Get them inside of you and then get them inside your children. Talk about them wherever you are, sitting at home or walking in the street; talk about them from the time you get up in the morning to when you fall into bed at night." Deut 6:6-8 (The Message)

It is imperative that you know how powerful God's Word is, not only knowing the truth in your heart but the power it has when you speak it out of your mouth.

Growing up isn't easy and being a teenager will always have its ups and downs, but I pray that this little book in your hands will help, encourage and guide you when you most need it. Recognise the Word of God is a weapon in your hand and a sword in your mouth.

"For we have the living Word of God, which is full of energy, and it pierces more sharply than a two-edged sword. It will even penetrate to the very core of our being where soul and spirit, bone and marrow meet! It interprets and reveals the true thoughts and secret motives of our hearts." *Hebrews 4:12 TPT*

Romans 12 promises that we can be "transformed by the renewing of our minds." I pray this book would utterly transform your world, as the power of God's Word hits your heart with creative force. May you never be the same again!

HOW TO USE BELIEVE & CONFESS

These declarations of faith have been grouped into 3 sections:

Section 1 looks at ourselves, focusing on our heart, mind, spirit, soul & body.

Section 2 focuses on who God is. If you want to know the will of God, you simply have to know the name of God – His will is His name. His name is His will. This section is grouped into days of the week for you to enjoy daily as part of your prayer times. Each declaration combines prayers, scriptures as you find them in the Bible, paraphrases for simple use, and personalisation of some verses so that you can confess them in the first person.

Don't feel like you have to stick to the days of the week. Speak which ever declaration you need for how you are feeling. For example: if you need comfort, head to **You Are ABBA** or if you're struggling with worry or anxiety go to section 1 and speak out the declaration on the **MIND** or **YOU ARE PEACE** from section 2.

I highly recommend repeating phrases that seem to have a particular resonance to you on particular days. If your spirit leaps at a certain phrase, speak it again and again while it feeds your soul. This is often the Holy Spirit at work releasing a fresh truth into your heart at some deeper level.

If you feel you want to move off into praise at some point, go with it! Don't feel you need to rigidly use these declarations – enjoy them; enjoy feasting on God's word, and thank Him for it!

Finally, at the end of the book in **section 3** you'll find a section called **WHO I AM**. These scriptures are listed reminding you who you are in Christ. When you are struggling with issues of identity, repeat these verses, speak them out, memorise them and embed them in your heart. You will also see a section called **WHAT TO READ IN TIME OF NEED**, this section connects God's Word with your emotions.

However you are feeling, let God's Word minister into your situation.

Mind

Spirit

Body

SECTION ONE

Heart

Soul

Heart

A GOOD MAN BRINGS GOOD THINGS OUT OF THE GOOD STORED UP IN HIS
HEART, AND AN EVIL MAN BRINGS EVIL THINGS OUT OF THE EVIL STORED UP I
HIS HEART. FOR THE MOUTH SPEAKS WHAT THE HEART IS FULL OF. LUKE 4:24

MY HEART [hahrt] *noun*

a person's centre for both physical and emotional-intellectual-moral activities*

Jesus, I bring You my heart. You say in Your Word, ***"the heart is dark and deceitful."*** But You God know my heart, and only You can penetrate it. Search me Lord, examine my mind, get straight to the root of the issue. ***"Create a new, clean heart within me. Fill me with pure thought and holy desires, ready to please You."*** *Psalm 51:10*

Help me Lord to protect and guard my heart, my innermost being, because from there flows the wellspring of life. I recognise life flows from my heart, and my life will reflect whatever state my heart is in. Therefore, I yield my heart to You. Take it and mould it, purify it so that I reflect Jesus.

Help me to put a guard on my mouth, so I don't lie or gossip. ***"Set a watch at the door of my lips. Don't let me so much as dream of evil or thoughtlessly fall into bad company."*** *Psalm 141:3 MSG* Help me to keep my eyes on You, with the truth of Your Word wrapped around my heart.

"I'm single-minded in pursuit of You; don't let me miss the road signs You've posted. I've banked Your promises in the vault of my heart so I won't sin myself bankrupt. Be blessed, God; train me in Your ways of wise living. I'll transfer to my lips all the counsel that comes from Your mouth; I delight far more in what You tell me about living than in gathering a pile of riches. I ponder every morsel of wisdom from You, I attentively watch how You've done it. I relish everything You've told me of life, I won't forget a word of it." *Psalm 119:9 (MSG)*

This declaration is based on the following scriptures: Jer 17:9-10; Prov 4:23,25; Prov 27:19; Prov 4:23,25; 2 Tim 3:14-17. (*biblestudytools.com)

Mind

STOP IMITATING THE IDEALS AND OPINIONS OF THE CULTURE AROUND YOU, BU[T]
BE INWARDLY TRANSFORMED BY THE HOLY SPIRIT THROUGH A TOTAL
REFORMATION OF HOW YOU THINK. THIS WILL EMPOWER YOU TO DISCERN GOD[S]
WILL AS YOU LIVE A BEAUTIFUL LIFE, SATISFYING AND PERFECT IN HIS EYES.
ROMANS 12:2 TPT

MY MIND [mahynd] *noun*

the element or complex of elements in an individual that feels, perceives, thinks, wills, and especially reasons*

Jesus, I give You my mind. I surrender every fear, every worry and every anxiety that I am currently experiencing. I choose to set my mind on You and not on earthly things.

"Whatever is true, whatever is honorable and worthy of respect, whatever is right and confirmed by God's word, whatever is pure and wholesome, whatever is lovely and brings peace, whatever is admirable and of good repute; if there is any excellence, if there is anything worthy of praise, think continually on these things [center your mind on them, and implant them in your heart]." *Philippians 4:8 (AMP)*

I refuse to give in to fear **"For God did not give <u>me</u> a spirit of timidity or cowardice or fear, but [He has given <u>me</u> a spirit] of power and of love and of sound judgment and personal discipline [abilities that result in a calm, well-balanced mind and self-control]."** *2 Tim1:7 (AMP)*

I recognise my mind is a battleground and I choose to take captive every thought and make it obedient to Christ. I direct my thoughts to Your Word, I meditate on it day and night. I choose to apply it to every area of my life and I will take time to listen to Your voice and walk in obedience to You.

This declaration is based on the following scriptures: John 14:1; Col 3:2; 2 Cor 10:5; Joshua 1:8 (*dictionary.cambridge.org)
(Altered words for personal confession are bold and underlined)

Spirit

"DEEP CALLS TO DEEP IN THE
ROAR OF YOUR WATERFALLS;
PSALM 42:7

MY SPIRIT [spir-it] *noun*

The spirit is that part of us that connects, or refuses to connect, to God. *

Jesus, fill me with Your Holy Spirit. Thank You that You are in me and I am in You. I drink deeply of Your Spirit within me.

Your Holy Spirit gives me life because You gave Your life. As You breathed life into Adam, breathe life into me. I yield to You.

Take hold of my humanity and empower me in my weakness. When I **"don't even know how to pray, or know the best things to ask for...the Holy Spirit rises up within <u>me</u> to super-intercede... in perfect harmony with God's plan and <u>my</u> destiny."** *Rom 8:26-28 (TPT)*

I choose to **"yield freely and fully to the dynamic life and power of the Holy Spirit"**, abandoning the desires of my flesh, allowing You to live freely within this body, this temple of the Holy Spirit.

I buy into the full freedom of the Spirit of grace, allowing You to lead me.

Thank You Jesus, Your Spirit empowers me and enables me. All I could ever need for life is found in Your Holy Spirit who is within me. Now I lift my hands and choose to worship You in spirit and in truth.

This declaration is based on the following scriptures: John 15; Eph 5:19; Gen 2:7; 1 John 4:13; Gal 5:16-18 TPT 2 Peter 1:3; John 4:23-24 (*researchgate. net) (Altered words for personal confession are bold and underlined)

Soul

WHY, MY SOUL, ARE YOU DOWNCAST? WHY SO DISTURBED WITHIN ME?
PUT YOUR HOPE IN GOD, FOR I WILL YET PRAISE HIM, MY SAVIOUR AND MY GOD
PSALM 42:11

MY SOUL [sohl] *noun*

*the part of you that consists of your mind, character, thoughts, and feelings.**

"What good will it be for someone to gain the whole world, yet forfeit their soul? Or what can anyone give in exchange for their soul?" *Matt 16:26 (NIV)*

Jesus, I give You my feelings and emotions. My highs, my lows, my successes and my failures, my ambitions and my pain. You are the source of my joy. When I gaze upon You, when I align my life with You, joy and fulfilment will overwhelm my soul.

I thirst and hunger after You. My soul craves You because I was made to be in relationship with You. Your love is better than life. As I lift my hands and surrender myself to You, wrap me in Your presence. Fill me and energise me with Your love.

"Truly my soul finds rest in God; my salvation comes from Him. Truly He is my rock and my salvation; He is my fortress, I shall never be shaken." *Psalm 62:1-2 (NIV)*

So, I speak to my soul and say, "Wake up! Worship God. Trust Him! Lean on Him. He will never fail you. God, **"You are my mountain of strength."** *Psalm 42:9 (TPT)*

"I sing in the shadow of Your wings. I cling to You; Your right hand upholds me." *Psalm 63:7-8 (NIV)*

This declaration is based on the following scriptures: Matt 5:6; Ps 43:5; Ps 42; Ps 63; Ps 62:1-2; Ps 57:8; Ps 42:9; (*collinsdictionary.com)

Body

"PRESENT YOUR BODIES A LIVING SACRIFICE, HOLY, ACCEPTABLE TO GOD, WHICH IS YOUR REASONABLE SERVICE. ROMANS 12:1 (NIV)

MY BODY [bod-ee] *noun*

the whole physical structure that forms a person*

Jesus, I give You my body. You tell me it is the temple of the Holy Spirit who is in me. You bought me at a price, and that price was the blood You shed on the cross. Thank You for giving Your life for mine.

Thank You that You made me in Your image God, therefore, You tell me I am a masterpiece and gloriously unique. You made me with purpose and destiny when You formed me in my mother's womb. I thank You that I am exquisite, I praise You, for I am fearfully and wonderfully made.

I choose to look through Your eyes and not from my own perspective. I choose to believe what You say about me, for You say I am chosen by You, out of darkness to experience Your marvelous light, and now You claim me as Your very own.

Your Word tell me that I will be a beautiful crown held high in the hand of Yahweh, a royal diadem of splendor in Your hands.

"Yahweh, You are **my** Father. We are like clay and You are our Potter. Each one of us is the creative, artistic work of Your hands." Isaiah 64:8 (TPT)

This declaration is based on the following scriptures: Gen 1:26-27; 1 Cor 6:19-20; Ephesians 2:10; Psalm 139:14; 1 Peter 2:9; Isaiah 62:3 TPT. (*dictionary. cambridge.org) (Altered words for personal confession are bold and underlined)

STOP IMITATING THE IDEALS AND OPINIONS OF
THE CULTURE AROUND YOU, BUT BE INWARDLY
TRANSFORMED BY THE HOLY SPIRIT THROUGH A
TOTAL REFORMATION OF HOW YOU THINK. THIS
WILL EMPOWER YOU TO DISCERN GOD'S WILL AS
YOU LIVE A BEAUTIFUL LIFE, SATISFYING AND
PERFECT IN HIS EYES.

ROMANS 12:2 TPT

The Way
The Truth
The Life
The Word
My Peace
Abba
The I Am

MONDAY: YOU ARE THE WAY

JESUS YOU ARE THE WAY

Today I choose to walk in Your ways. I will not be influenced by bad company, but instead allow Your Word to be my guide. It is my daily nourishment and quenches my thirst.

"Teach me Your way, LORD, that I may rely on Your faithfulness; give me an undivided heart, that I may fear Your name." Psalm 86:11

Thank You Jesus that because of Your sacrifice on the cross, You have made a way so that I can be in divine relationship with my Maker and Creator. There is no other way to God except through You.

Thank You for saving me from my wayward state and joining me to Yourself. Thank You for forgiving me of my sins and wiping the slate clean.

Even though the way ahead to me is unknown, I thank You that You know the plans You have for me and they are plans to prosper me and not to harm me, plans to give me a hope and a future. When I trust in You, I know You will show me the right way to go.

"How can a young person stay on the path of purity? By living according to Your word."
Psalm 119: 9

I choose to let Your Word guide me for *"Your word is a lamp for my feet, a light on my path."*
Psalm 119:105

Even when I go through difficult seasons You have promised that You will be with me, You will not hide from me but I will hear Your voice guiding me saying, **"This is the right path; follow it."**

You know my needs before I even ask and when I seek first Your Kingdom and righteousness, you promised, **"all these things shall be added to <u>me</u>."** Matthew 6:32-33.

I thank You that Your Word says, **"The lovers of God who chase after righteousness will find all their dreams come true: an abundant life drenched with favor and a fountain that overflows with satisfaction."** Proverbs 21:21 TPT

So I commit my way to You Lord; I trust in You, and I thank You knowing You will keep Your Word. All Your promises are "yes" and "amen."

I give you thanks and praise and worship You for all that You are and all that You are going to do.

You are the Way and I choose to follow You, my Lord, My King, My Saviour!

This declaration is based on the following scriptures: John 14:6; Psalm 1; Romans 3:22-26; 1 John 1:7: 2:1;Psalm 51; 103:1-5; Isaiah 1:18; Jer 29: 11; Prov 3:5-6; Psalm 119: 9; Isaiah 30:20-23; Proverbs 21:21; Psalm 37:5; 2 Cor 1:20 *(Altered words for personal confession are bold and underlined)*

TUESDAY: YOU ARE THE TRUTH

JESUS YOU ARE THE TRUTH

Jesus, I thank You that You are the truth and Your truth has set me free. I embrace the reality of Christ as it brings more and more freedom into my life.

I stand firm in my faith *"with the belt of truth buckled around <u>my</u> waist, with the breastplate of righteousness in place."* Eph 6:14

"Your Word is truth!" John 17:17 (TPT) and all your promises are yes and amen. Guide me in Your truth, help me to hear Your voice and walk in Your ways.

I choose not to believe the lies spoken from others or the feelings that speak untruths, but I choose to believe what Your Word says about me. Satan is a liar and the father of lies, but Your truth shows me my true identity. I look at Your Word like a mirror and see my identity is in You.

"I am fearfully and wonderfully made" Psalm 139:14 (NKJV)

I am a royal jewel in Your hand. I am a child of God, a royal heir of Your Kingdom. You say, **"Everything I have is yours"**.

God, help me to see from Your perspective, through Your eyes, for You have raised me up and seated me with Christ, a place of perfection and authority. You are the God who sees me.

You say I am chosen, righteous and holy. Because of Jesus I can stand in Your presence. Your Holy Spirit has made His home in me.

"Lord, who dares to dwell with You? Who presumes the privilege of being close to You, living next to You in Your shining place of glory? Who are those who daily dwell in the life of the Holy Spirit? They are passionate and wholehearted, always sincere and always speaking the truth—for their hearts are trustworthy. They refuse to slander or insult others; they'll never listen to gossip or rumors, nor would they ever harm another with their words. They will speak out passionately against evil and evil workers while commending the faithful ones who follow after the truth. They make firm commitments and follow through, even at great cost. They never crush others with exploitation or abuse and they would never be bought with a bribe against the innocent. They will never be shaken; they will stand firm forever." Psalm 15:1-5 TPT

Thank You for the truth of Your Word. Let it permeate every fibre of my being.

This declaration is based on the following scriptures: John 8:32; Eph 6:14; 2 Cor 1:20; John 16:13; John 8:44; Isaiah 62:3; James 2:5; (Luke 15:31); (Ephesians 2:6-7; Gen 16:13; 2 Cor 5:21; Eph 3:17 *(Altered words for personal confession are bold and underlined)*

WEDNESDAY: YOU ARE THE LIFE

JESUS YOU ARE THE LIFE

You are the Resurrection and the Life.

I was dead in my sin, but You have made me alive in You. *"You lifted me out of the pit of despair, out of the mud and the mire. You set my feet on solid ground and steadied me as I walked along." Psalm 40:2 (NLT)*

"Everything we could ever need for life and complete devotion, God has already been deposited in us by His divine power. For all this was lavished upon us through the rich experience of knowing Him who has called us by name and invited us to come to Him through a glorious manifestation of His goodness." 2 Peter 1:3 (TPT)

Thank You that Your grace helps me to live for You. For You tell me, *"My grace is sufficient for you, for My strength is made perfect in weakness." 2 Cor 12:9* It is by grace I am saved. It is a gift from You.

Jesus, thank You for giving Your life, so that I could live my best life! You gave Your life so that I can be healed! You gave Your life so that I can be set free. You gave Your life so that I can live in victory.

"Yes, God raised Jesus to life! And since God's Spirit of Resurrection lives in me, He will also raise my body to life by the same Spirit that breathes life into me!" Romans 8:11 (TPT)

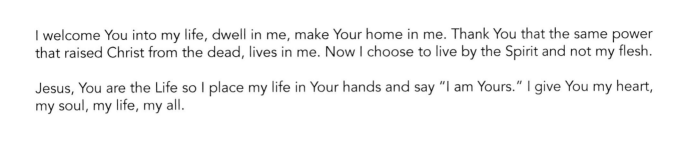

I welcome You into my life, dwell in me, make Your home in me. Thank You that the same power that raised Christ from the dead, lives in me. Now I choose to live by the Spirit and not my flesh.

Jesus, You are the Life so I place my life in Your hands and say "I am Yours." I give You my heart, my soul, my life, my all.

This declaration is based on the following scriptures: John 11:25; Eph 2; eph2 2:8; Isaiah 53:5; Gal 5:1; 1 Cor 15:57; Rom 8:11
(Altered words for personal confession are bold and underlined)

THURSDAY: YOU ARE THE WORD

JESUS YOU ARE THE WORD

Your Word is life to me, this covenant and this relationship means everything to me. You are my God, my Lord, my Master, my Deliverer and I worship You. Lord, give me the Spirit of wisdom and revelation right now, so that I may know You better. Enlighten my eyes to know Your hope, Your inheritance for me and Your incomparably great power, available to me today.

I choose to speak Your Word because it is powerful, it is quick, sharp and active. The Word of God in my mouth is as powerful as it is coming from Yours. I put a guard on my mouth because I know my words are powerful.

Your word brings life and light, it *"is a lamp for my feet,* and *a light on my path." Psalm 119:105* It is perfect in every way; it revives my soul and leads me to truth.

"I prize God's word like others prize the finest gold. Nothing brings the soul such sweetness as seeking His living words." Psalm 19:10 (TPT)

Your word gives me wisdom. When I lack understanding or direction, Your Word directs me and keeps me from sin.

Your Word empowers me for *"Every Scripture has been written by the Holy Spirit, the breath of God. It will empower me by its instruction and correction, giving me the strength to take the right direction and lead me deeper into the path of godliness." 2 Tim 3:16 (TPT)*

Your Word heals. Just say the word and I will be healed.

Jesus, You are the Word…You were there in the beginning.

"The Word was with God, and the Word was God. He existed in the beginning with God. God created everything through Him, and nothing was created except through Him. The Word gave life to everything that was created, and his life brought light to everyone. The light shines in the darkness, and the darkness can never extinguish it." John 1:1-5 (NLT)

I am blessed when I walk in Your Word and when I hide Your Word in my heart.
I choose to let Your Word dwell in me and nourish me. I meditate on it day and night.

Thank You for this incredible gift. What a privilege You have given me that I can access the living, breathing Word of God.

This declaration is based on the following scriptures: Eph 1:17-23; Heb 4:12; Psalm 141:3; Psalm 119:130-136; Psalm 19; Psalm 119:133; 2 Timothy 3:16 (TPT); Psalm 107:20; Psalm 119:1-4; 11. Psalm 1:2; Col 3:16 (Altered words for personal confession are bold and underlined)

FRIDAY: YOU ARE PEACE

YOU ARE MY PEACE

Heavenly Father, I have the perfect peace of God. ***"Peace which reassures the heart, peace which transcends all understanding, that peace which stands guard over my heart and my mind in Christ Jesus."*** *Phil 4:7 (AMP)*

Peace that the world can not understand. I walk with inner peace because the spoken words of Jesus have their home in me.

I refuse to be anxious. I am not and will not be intimidated. I will not fear people who are against me. I will not agonise or get upset. Instead I will pray. Sculpting my anxiety into prayers, praise and petitions before God.

You tell me, ***"do not fear [anything], for I am with you; do not be afraid, for I am your God. I will strengthen you, be assured I will help you; I will certainly take hold of you with My righteous right hand [a hand of justice, of power, of victory, of salvation]."*** *Is 41:10 (AMP)*

I choose to focus my mind on You. I choose to stay in constant peace trusting in You with confidence and expectation. You are ***"not a God of confusion and disorder but of peace and order."*** *1 Cor 14:33 (AMP)*

I know that You cause ***"everything to work together for the good of those who love God and are called according to His purpose."*** *Rom 8:28 (NLT)*

I trust in You my Lord, with all of my heart. I will not rely on my own understanding but I align myself with Your word, with Your truth and wait calmly with inner peace, knowing You will give me direction. Because You are with me, I never shall be shaken. No weapon formed against me can succeed. No harm will befall me.

I will focus on things that are true, noble, right, pure, lovely, admirable, excellent and praise worthy. I will not be distracted. And the God of peace will be with me. I will fix my mind on You - and You will keep me in perfect peace.

Whatever battle I go through, Your promise is that You will crush Satan under Your feet.
You are my Saviour, a Warrior, my Father.

I will both lie down in peace, and sleep; For You alone O Lord, make me dwell in safety.

You are my fortress, my shield, my banner, my everlasting rock. You are my dwelling place. My hiding place. My home. You are Jehovah El Shaddai - the God who is more than enough.

You are the Alpha and Omega, the first and the last, who was and is and is to come. Thank You, You have given me Your peace.

Confession based on the following scriptures: Eph 1:17-23; Judges 6:24; Rom 8:6; Rom 5:1; Col 3:15-16; Phil 4:6; Ps 1:2-3; Ps 3:5-6; Is 26:3-4; Prov 3:5-6

SATURDAY: YOU ARE ABBA

YOU ARE ABBA

You are a good and perfect father. You are unaffected by human frailties.

You know me completely, inside and out. Your thoughts about me outweigh the grains of sand. You are obsessed with me.

You are always with me, You never leave me. You have adopted me as your child. I am Yours and You are mine.

You are my shepherd, my comforter, my guide. You are my provider. I lack nothing. All that I need is in You. Every craving can be satisfied in You. You are a God of extravagance. A God of wealth. Rich in grace and mercy.

"Even when I must walk through the darkest valley, I fear no danger, for You are with me; Your rod and Your staff reassure me. You prepare a feast before me in plain sight of my enemies.You refresh my head with oil; my cup is completely full. Surely Your goodness and faithfulness will pursue me all my days, and I will live in the Lord's house for the rest of my life." Psalm 23:4-6 (NET)

Thank You Heavenly Father. I love You and worship Your wonderful name.

This declaration is based on the following scriptures: Psalm 139; Rom 8:15; Psalm 23

SUNDAY: YOU ARE THE I AM

YOU ARE THE GREAT I AM

You are the great *"I AM WHO I AM." Ex 3:14* As You were with Moses, You will be with me.

Your name reveals Your nature. You are Healer, You are Provider, You are Shield. You WILL BE all that I need You to be.

Your Word says...

"I will bless those who bless you" Genesis 12:3 (NIV)

"I will make you very fruitful" Genesis17:6 (NIV)

"I will help you speak and will teach you what to say." Exodus 4:12 (NIV)

"My Presence will go with you, and I will give you rest." Exodus 33:14 (NIV)

"I will cause all My goodness to pass in front of you, and I will proclaim My name, the LORD, in your presence. I will have mercy on whom I will have mercy, and I will have compassion on whom I will have compassion."** Exodus 33:19 (NIV)

"I will give you every place where you set your foot, as I promised Moses."** Joshua 1:3 (NIV)

"I will be his father, and he will be My son. I will never take My love away from him." 1 Chronicles 17:13 (NIV)

"I will deliver you" 2 Kings 20:6 (NIV)

"I will instruct you and teach you in the way you should go; I will counsel you with My loving eye on you." Psalm 32:8 (NIV)

"I will rescue him; I will protect him, for he acknowledges My name. He will call on Me, and I will answer him; I will be with him in trouble, I will deliver him and honour him. With long life I will satisfy him and show him My salvation." Psalm 91:14-16 (NIV)

"I will make rivers flow on barren heights, and springs within the valleys. I will turn the desert into pools of water, and the parched ground into springs." Isaiah 41:18 (NIV)

"I will put My Spirit on him"

"I will take hold of your hand. I will keep you"

"I will lead the blind by ways they have not known, along unfamiliar paths I will guide them; I will turn the darkness into light before them and make the rough places smooth." Isaiah 42:1, 6, 16 (NIV)

"I will go before you and will level the mountains; I will break down gates of bronze and cut through bars of iron. I will give you hidden treasures, riches stored in secret places"

"I will strengthen you" Isaiah 45:2-3, 5 (NIV)

"I will carry you; I will sustain you and I will rescue you." Isaiah 46:4 (NIV)

"I will refresh the weary and satisfy the faint." Jeremiah 31:25 (NIV)

"I will make an everlasting covenant with <u>you</u>: I will never stop doing good to <u>you</u>, and I will inspire <u>you</u> to fear me, so that <u>you</u> will never turn away from Me. I will rejoice in doing <u>you</u> good and will assuredly plant <u>you</u> in this land with all My heart and soul." Jeremiah 32:40-41 (NIV)

"I will bring health and healing to it; I will heal My people and will let them enjoy abundant peace and security." Jeremiah 33:6 (NIV)

"I will make them and the places surrounding my hill a blessing. I will send down showers in season; there will be showers of blessing." Ezekiel 34:26 (NIV)

"I will save you from all your uncleanness. I will call for the grain and make it plentiful and will not bring famine upon you. **I will increase the fruit of the trees and the crops of the field**, so that you will no longer suffer disgrace among the nations because of famine." Ezekiel 36:29-30 (NIV)

"I will make a covenant of peace with them; it will be an everlasting covenant. **I will establish them and increase their numbers, and I will put my sanctuary among them forever**. My dwelling place will be with them; **I will be their God**, and they will be My people." Ezekiel 37:26-27 (NIV)

"I will deliver this people from the power of the grave; I will redeem them from death." Hosea 13:14 (NIV)

"I will make you fishers of men" Matt 4:19 (NKJ)

"I will give you rest." Matthew 11:28 (NIV)

"I will go ahead of you" Matthew 26:32 (NIV)

Thank You God that You will make me fruitful, You will protect me, You will sustain me, You will guide me, You will heal me, You will help me, You will make me, You will go ahead of me.

Thank You for Your promises. Thank You that Your Word will never return to You unfulfilled.

(Altered words for personal confession are bold and underlined)

I am healed

I am loved

I am chosen

SECTION THREE

I am forgiven

I am saved

I am a new crea

WHO I AM IN CHRIST

The following list of scriptures compiled by Joyce Meyer ministries reveals the truth about who God created you to be. I encourage you to meditate on each of these scriptures and speak out the declarations written in bold.

I am complete in Him Who is the head over all rule and authority—of every angelic and earthly power (Colossians 2:10).

I am alive with Christ (Ephesians 2:5).

I am free from the law of sin and death (Romans 8:2).

I am far from oppression, and I will not live in fear (Isaiah 54:14).

I am born of God, and the evil one does not touch me (1 John 5:18).

I am holy and without blame before Him in love (Ephesians 1:4; 1 Peter 1:16).

I have the mind of Christ (1 Corinthians 2:16; Philippians 2:5).

I have the peace of God that surpasses all understanding (Philippians 4:7).

The Spirit of God, who is greater than the enemy in the world, lives in me (1 John 4:4).

I have received abundant grace and the gift of righteousness and reign in life through Jesus Christ (Romans 5:17).

I have received the Spirit of wisdom and revelation in the knowledge of Jesus, the eyes of my heart enlightened, so that I know the hope of having life in Christ (Ephesians 1:17-18).

I have received the power of the Holy Spirit and He can do miraculous things through me, **I have**

authority and power over the enemy in this world (Mark 16:17-18; Luke 10:17-19).

I am merciful, I do not judge others, and **I forgive quickly**. As I do this by God's grace, He blesses my life (Luke 6:36-38).

God supplies all of my needs according to His riches in glory in Christ Jesus (Philippians 4:19).

In all circumstances **I live by faith in God and extinguish all the flaming darts (attacks) of the enemy** (Ephesians 6:16).

I can do whatever I need to do in life through Christ Jesus who gives me strength (Philippians 4:13).

I am chosen by God who called me out of the darkness of sin and into the light and life of Christ so I can proclaim the excellence and greatness of who He is (1 Peter 2:9).

I am born again—spiritually transformed, renewed and set apart for God's purpose—through the living and everlasting word of God (1 Peter 1:23).

I am God's workmanship, created in Christ to do good works that He has prepared for me to do (Ephesians 2:10).

I am a new creation in Christ (2 Corinthians 5:17).

In Christ, I am dead to sin—my relationship to it is broken—and alive to God—living in unbroken fellowship with Him (Romans 6:11).

The light of God's truth has shone in my heart and given me knowledge of salvation through Christ (2 Corinthians 4:6).

As I hear God's Word, I do what it says and I am blessed in my actions (James 1:22, 25).

I am a joint-heir with Christ (Romans 8:17). **I am more than a conqueror through Him who loves me** (Romans 8:37).

I overcome the enemy of my soul by the blood of the Lamb and the word of my testimony (Revelation 12:11).

I have everything I need to live a godly life and am equipped to live in His divine nature (2 Peter 1:3-4).

I am an ambassador for Christ (2 Corinthians 5:20). **I am part of a chosen generation, a royal priesthood, a holy nation, a purchased people** (1 Peter 2:9).

I am the righteousness of God—I have right standing with Him—**in Jesus Christ** (2 Corinthians 5:21).

My body is a temple of the Holy Spirit; I belong to Him (1 Corinthians 6:19).

I am the head and not the tail, and I only go up and not down in life as I trust and obey God (Deuteronomy 28:13).

I am the light of the world (Matthew 5:14).

I am chosen by God, forgiven and justified through Christ. I have a compassionate heart, kindness, humility, meekness and patience (Romans 8:33; Colossians 3:12).

I am redeemed—forgiven of all my sins and made clean—through the blood of Christ (Ephesians 1:7).

I have been rescued from the domain and the power of darkness and brought into God's kingdom (Colossians 1:13).

I am redeemed from the curse of sin, sickness, and poverty (Deuteronomy 28:15-68; Galatians 3:13).

My life is rooted in my faith in Christ and I overflow with thanksgiving for all He has done for me (Colossians 2:7).

I am called to live a holy life by the grace of God and to declare His praise in the world (Psalm

66:8; 2 Timothy 1:9).

I am healed and whole in Jesus (Isaiah 53:5; 1 Peter 2:24).

I am saved by God's grace, raised up with Christ and seated with Him in heavenly places (Ephesians 2:5-6; Colossians 2:12).

I am greatly loved by God (John 3:16; Ephesians 2:4; Colossians 3:12; 1 Thessalonians 1:4).

I am strengthened with all power according to His glorious might (Colossians 1:11).

I humbly submit myself to God, and the devil flees from me because I resist him in the Name of Jesus (James 4:7).

I press on each day to fulfill God's plan for my life because I live to please Him (Philippians 3:14).

I am not ruled by fear because the Holy Spirit lives in me and gives me His power, love and self-control (2 Timothy 1:7).

Christ lives in me, and I live by faith in Him and His love for me (Galatians 2:20).

https://joycemeyer.org/everydayanswers/ea-teachings/knowing-who-i-am-in-christ

WHAT TO READ IN TIME OF NEED

WHEN I'M WORRIED...........................MATTHEW 11:28-30
WHEN I'M ANXIOUS................................. 1 PETER 5:7
WHEN I'M DEPRESSED..................PSALM 9:9; PSALM 23
WHEN IM STRESSED................................PSALM 34:4-5
WHEN I'M LONELY................................ROMANS 8:31-39
WHEN I'M TEMPTED...........................JAMES 1:13-18
WHEN I'M IN A RELATIONSHIP.......................2 COR 6:14
WHEN I'M IN POVERTY..........................PSALM 34:6
WHEN I FEEL SUICIDAL.................................JOHN 10:10
WHEN I FEEL FAR FROM GOD..................PSALM 139:7-9
WHEN I AM BRIEVED...........................PSALM 147:3
WHEN I AM SAD...............................PSALM 43:5
WHEN I'M JEALOUS.............................PROVERBS 14:30
WHEN I'M ANGRY.....................COL 3:8; EPH 4:26
WHEN I'M SORRY.........................1 JOHN 1:9; PSALM 32:5
WHEN I STRUGGLE TO FORGIVE.................MATT 6:14-15
WHN I'M BULLIED............................LUKE 6:27-28
WHEN I'M LIED TO................................MATT 5:11-21
WHEN I FEEL UGLY..............................PSALM 139:13-14
WHEN I FEEL UPSET..............................PSALM 34:18
WHEN I LOSE FRIENDS..........................PROVERBS 18:24

WHEN I'M DISCOURAGED................................ISAIAH 40
WHEN I HAVE SINNED...............................PSALM 51
WHEN I'M IN DANGER.............................PSALM 91
WHEN I NEED COURAGE...............................JOSHUA 1
WHEN I FEEL CRITICAL...............................1 COR 13
WHEN I'M IN SORROW................................JOHN 14
WHEN I'M FEARFUL...............................PSALM 56
WHEN THE WORLD SEEMS BIGGER THAN GOD......PS 90
WHEN I HAVE THE BLUES...............................PSALM 34
WHEN PEOPLE FAIL ME................................PSALM 27
WHEN FEEL WEAK................................2 COR 12:9
WHEN I LACK FAITH................................2 TIM 2:13
WHEN I'M IN NEED................................PHIL 4:19
WHEN THINGS DON'T GO TO PLAN.................ROM 8:28
WHEN I NEED HEALING................................1 PETER 2:24
WHEN I'M CONFUSED............................PROVERBS 3:5-6
WHN I FEEL LOST................................ISAIAH 30:21
WHEN I'M IN DOUBT................................JAMES 1:5-8
WHEN I'M STRUGGLING.................ISAIAH 41:10
WHEN I'M SCARED................................2 TIM 1:7
WHEN I'M TIRED................................PHIL 4:13

GOD is...
ABBA
Beginning
Comforter
DELIVERER
Emmanuel
Faithful & True

GOD IS...

Daniel 11:32b says *"Those who know their God shall be valiant and do great exploits!"*

Knowing God leads to incredible strength and bravery. The Bible shows us that we know God through His Name. Here's some wonderful truths about God's incredible Name:

Firstly, He reveals Himself through many names, names that mean things like: *"The Lord my sanctifier," "The Lord my shepherd," "The Lord who is present," "The Lord our healer," "The Lord our righteousness," "The Lord will provide," "The Lord is peace," "The Lord of Hosts," "The God of Recompense," "The Most High God," "The strong One who sees," "The everlasting God."*

Now let me give you an A-Z of God's Names and character traits from Bible.

THE AVENGER..Thess.4:6
ABBA...Romans 8:15
ADVOCATE...I John 2:1 (kjv)
ALMIGHTY...Genesis 17:1
ALL IN ALL..Colossians 3:11
ANCIENT OF DAYS...Daniel 7:9
ANOINTED ONE...Psalm 2:2
ARM OF THE LORD...Isaiah 53:1
AUTHOR OF ETERNAL SALVATION..............Hebrews 5:9
AUTHOR OF OUR FAITH...........................Hebrews 12:2
AUTHOR OF PEACE....................................1 Cor. 14:33
BEGINNING...Revelation 21:6
BISHOP OF SOULS.......................................1 Peter 2:25

BREAD OF GOD...John 6:33
BREAD OF LIFE...John 6:35
BREATH OF LIFE...............Genesis 2:7, Revelation 11:11
BRIDEGROOM..Isaiah 62:5
BRIGHT MORNING STAR.......................Revelation 22:16
CAPTAIN OF SALVATION........................Hebrews 2:10
COMFORTER..John 14:26(kjv)
CONSUMING FIRE.......................Deut. 4:24, Heb. 12:29
CORNERSTONE...Isaiah 28:16
COUNSELLOR..Isaiah 9:6
CREATOR...1 Peter 4:19
CROWN OF BEAUTY.......................................Isaiah 28:5
DAYSPRING...Luke 1:78

DELIVERER...Romans 11:26
DESIRED OF ALL NATIONS............................Haggai 2:7
DIADEM OF BEAUTY...................................Isaiah 28:5
DOOR...John 10:7(kjv)
DWELLING PLACE.....................................Psalm 90:1
EMMANUEL.......................................Matthew 1:23(kjv)
DELIVERER...Romans 11:26
DESIRED OF ALL NATIONS............................Haggai 2:7
DIADEM OF BEAUTY...................................Isaiah 28:5
DOOR...John 10:7(kjv)
DWELLING PLACE.....................................Psalm 90:1
EMMANUEL.......................................Matthew 1:23(kjv)
GOD WITH US, EVERLASTING FATHER............Isaiah 9:6
FAITHFUL & TRUE......................................Revelation 19:11
FATHER..Matthew 6:9
FORTRESS..Jeremiah 16:19
FOUNDATION..1 Cor. 3:11
FOUNTAIN OF LIVING WATERS.................Jeremiah 2:13
FRIEND..Matthew 11:19
GENTLE WHISPER...................................1 Kings 19:12
GIFT OF GOD..John 4:10
GOD WHO SEES ME..................................Genesis 16:13
GOOD SHEPHERD.....................................John 10:11
GREAT HIGH PRIEST.................................Hebrews 4:14
GUIDE..Psalm 48:14
HEAD OF THE CHURCH............................Ephesians 5:23
HIDING PLACE..Psalm 32:7
JUDGE.............................Isaiah 33:22, Acts 10:42
KEEPER..Psalm 121:5
KING..Zechariah 9:9
LAMB OF GOD..John 1:29

LAST ADAM..1 Cor. 15:45
LAWGIVER...Isaiah 33:22
LEADER..Isaiah 55:4
LIFE..John 14:6
LIGHT OF THE WORLD................................John 8:12
LION OF THE TRIBE OF JUDAH.................Revelation 5:5
LIVING WATER..John 4:10
MASTER..Luke 5:5
MEDIATOR..1 Timothy 2:5
MERCIFUL GOD.......................................Jeremiah 3:12
MESSENGER OF THE COVENANT................Malachi 3:1
OUR PASSOVER LAMB.................................1 Cor. 5:7
OUR PEACE..Ephesians 2:14
PHYSICIAN...Luke 4:23
PORTION...........................Psalm 73:26, Psalm 119:57
POTTER..Isaiah 64:8
PRINCE OF LIFE...Acts 3:15
PRINCE OF PEACE.....................................Isaiah 9:6
PROPHET..Acts 3:22
PURIFIER..Malachi 3:3
QUICKENING SPIRIT.....................1 Corinthians 15:45(kjv)
RABBONI (TEACHER)...................................John 20:16
RADIANCE OF GOD'S GLORY...........................Heb.1:3
REDEEMER..Job 19:25
REFINER'S FIRE..Malachi 3:2
REFUGE...Jeremiah 16:19
RESURRECTION...John 11:25
REWARDER...Hebrews 11:6
RIGHTEOUS ONE......................................1 John 2:1
ROCK..1 Cor.10:4
SAVIOUR..Luke 2:11

I don't think there is a thing in this world that God cannot be to you!

He made you, to love you. So let Him!

BELIEVE *Confess*

Believe and Confess has grown from a single daily confession book to a series of books and daily devotions. We continue to get wonderful testimonies of how this series has helped so many of all ages.

Believe and Confess is also now on Instagram & YouTube. Follow the links to receive Believe & Confess devotions every weekday.

https://www.instagram.com/vickytorico/channel/
https://www.youtube.com/jarrodlcoopertv

OUR BELIEVE & CONFESS BOOKS

Believe & Confess By Jarrod & Victoria Cooper

For many years, Vicky has used a wonderful book of daily confessions of faith. Often times, whether in a battle season, or simply as daily devotions, I have seen her pour over the confessions – whispering them into her own spirit and mind. Again and again I would see her eyes brighten, her worship deepen, her sense of God and dignity strengthen – all by spending a few minutes daily polishing her faith and focus for the day ahead.

It is because of the power of such confessions that we offer you this book, teaching why confession is powerful and necessary, how you can use it to change your mind and your world – and then leaving you with confessions for each day, for regular use. Romans 12 promises that we can be "transformed by the renewing of our minds". We pray this book would utterly transform your world, as the power of God's word hits your heart with creative force. May you never be the same again!

ALSO AVAILABLE AS A GROUP DISCUSSION BOOK

Believe & Confess FOR KIDS By Victoria Cooper

These short, simple declarations are all based on scripture using a combination of prayers and paraphrases from various translations of the Bible. There are seven different declarations, grouped into days of the week so they can be used daily or used specifically to target a situation or emotion your child is feeling. The word of God is powerful, the Bible says that it is like "a two edged sword" in our mouth (Heb 4:12/Psalm 149:6), so it is important to help and guide our children to use it effectively and not just to see the Bible as a story book.

When my son Zach was 9 years old, he used to get really scared at night. Every time he went to bed his imagination would run wild and make him very fearful for no reason. This book started when I wrote out a declaration for him to say every night before going to sleep. Sometimes he would speak it out 2 or 3 times a night until he knew it off-by-heart and the fear left him.

Ben Gets Scared By Zachary Cooper

As part of the Believe & Confess Series, Zach Cooper has added his own contribution with a storybook for kids about conquering fear with the Word of God.

This is a story about a boy who is scared of heights, scared of spiders and scared at night. Join Ben as he discovers a very special way to fight his fears.

Suitable for children aged 3+

If you are inspired by the ministry of Jarrod and Victoria Cooper and want to stay connected, why not join our online community of passionate learners, leaders and churches across the world, dedicated to growing in God, growing in skills for life and leadership and growing in God's presence and power for revival.

There are currently three levels of Tribe membership:

Tier 1 – LEARN (Access to our growing online digital library)
Tier 2 – LEAD: Global Leadership Tribe (or GLT for short.)
Tier 3 – LEAD+ (Group access for up to 10 leaders)

Membership includes:

- Unlimited access to all our online courses and extensive library of video and audio teachings.
- Free books
- Private webinars, teaching series and online coaching sessions.
- Private Facebook group to interact closely with Jarrod, Vicky and other tribe members.

Visit JarrodCooper.net/join-our-tribe for more information

DOWNLOAD OUR FREE APP

Are you feeling uninspired spiritually? Need a fresh daily devotional? Are you ready to move beyond the stress, anxiety, and weariness of this rollercoaster year? Are you looking for fresh clarity and confidence in God for the years ahead? Do you want to connect with people who are prophetic, with a proven 30-year track-record in lifting, inspiring and bringing hope and faith to lives, and releasing people into fresh God-encounters?

We have good news for you! Jarrod & Victoria Cooper's new, free, TRIBE app will bring you:

- Daily faith filled devotionals
- Teaching broadcasts
- Prophetic words
- Worship
- Podcasts
- Regular Livestreamed events

All FREE OF CHARGE to your app, with the ability to upgrade your subscription to the global online learning community and team mentoring tiers of THE TRIBE if desired – but no pressure, just enjoy the free stuff above by all means!

Simply download the app to your smartphone today and start being inspired straight away!

Head to JarrodCooper.net/app or scan this QR code with your smartphone to download.

About Victoria Cooper

@VICKYTORICO

Victoria is married to Jarrod Cooper who is the Senior Leader of Revive Church, a growing church based in East Yorkshire. As well as being an author, Vicky has a passion for Presence-filled creativity that touches the hearts of everyone! With experience in dance, and having overseen productions, concerts and shows that have been touched by God's presence and that have led many to Christ, Vicky's heart to coach creatives to fullness in God, will inspire you through her work.

Follow Victoria on:
Instagram: @vickytorico
Twitter: @vickytorico
Facebook: facebook.com/vickytorico
YouTube: youtube.com/jarrodlcoopertv

Visit JarrodCooper.Net

To keep up to date with news from Jarrod & Vicky or to purchase their products visit their website
www.jarrodcooper.net

Printed in Great Britain
by Amazon

66649624R00030